Wild animals

Los animales salvajes

lohs ah-nee-*mah*-lehs sahl-*vah*-hehs

Illustrated by Clare Beaton

Ilustraciones de Clare Beaton

BARRON'S

hippopotamus

el hipopótamo

ehl ee-poh-*poh*-tah-moh

elephant

el elefante

ehl eh-leh-*fahn*-teh

lion

el león

ehl leh-*ohn*

polar bear

el oso polar

ehl *oh*-soh poh-*lahr*

tiger

el tigre

ehl *tee*-greh

monkey

el mono

ehl *moh*-noh

zebra

la cebra

lah *seh*-brah

crocodile

el cocodrilo

ehl koh-koh-*dree*-loh

kangaroo

el canguro

ehl kahn-*goo*-roh

giraffe

la jirafa

lah hee-*rah*-fah

snake

la serpiente

lah sehr-pee-*ehn*-teh

A simple guide to pronouncing the Spanish words*

- Read this guide as naturally as possible, as if it were English.
- Put stress on the letters in *italics* e.g. ehl eh-leh-*fahn*-teh.

el hipopótamo	ehl ee-poh-*poh*-tah-moh	**hippopotamus**
el elefante	ehl eh-leh-*fahn*-teh	**elephant**
el león	ehl leh-*ohn*	**lion**
el oso polar	ehl *oh*-soh poh-*lahr*	**polar bear**
el tigre	ehl *tee*-greh	**tiger**
el mono	ehl *moh*-noh	**monkey**
la cebra	lah *seh*-brah	**zebra**
el cocodrilo	ehl koh-koh-*dree*-loh	**crocodile**
el canguro	ehl kahn-*goo*-roh	**kangaroo**
la jirafa	lah hee-*rah*-fah	**giraffe**
la serpiente	lah sehr-pee-*ehn*-teh	**snake**

*There are many different guides to pronunciation. Our guide attempts to balance precision with simplicity.

Text and illustrations © Copyright 2002 by B SMALL PUBLISHING, Surrey England.
First edition for the United States, its Dependencies, Canada, and the Philippines published in 2002 by Barron's Educational Series, Inc.
All rights reserved. No part of this book may be reproduced in any form, by photostat, microfilm, xerography, or any other means, or incorporated into any information retrieval system, electronic or mechanical, without the written permission of the copyright owner.
Address all inquiries to: Barron's Educational Series, Inc., 250 Wireless Boulevard, Hauppauge, New York 11788.
(http://www.barronseduc.com)
ISBN-13: 978-0-7641-2213-2   ISBN-10: 0-7641-2213-4
Library of Congress Catalog Card Number 2001099157
Printed in China   9 8 7 6 5 4 3